yo

akhira

your name hurts

independently published

ISBN: 9798857089897

instagram.com/dyingful
instagram.com/akhirapoetry
twitter.com/akhirapoetry
tiktok.com/@akhirapoetry

when you left
you didn't only destroy me
you destroyed words, places,
songs and names

you stopped saying your goodnights
and that's when i knew i lost you

i say it's your loss
but deep down
i know it's mine too

you seemed so interested
could you tell me
was it real
or was it all in my head?

it still hurts sometimes
because i loved you so much
and it didn't work out

when you look at me
do you see
the person you loved
or the person you left?

how do you tell someone
that the reason you're sad
is because you love them?

i will never regret you
or say that i wish
i'd never met you

because once upon
a time, you were
exactly what i needed

i still go back
and look at
the messages
you left on read
wondering if
there were something
else i could have said
to make you stay

you will never even know
how much i cried over you

i never stopped loving you
i only started pretending i don't

remember how we
used to talk everyday?

- *yeah i miss that*

seeing you will always hurt

it hurts to remember
how close we were
back then

we were never
meant for each other
but i'm glad that
for a moment
it felt like we were

why don't you look at me
the same way you used to?

i talk about you like
you still haven't left yet

you never apologized
to me for hurting me,
but i apologized 12 times
for being angry about it

but how do you say
goodbye when your
heart still wants to hold
on?

and we didn't see each other
after that

you only realize
how much you love
someone
when one day
they don't love you back

i just cried my eyes over you
and i still wanna be with you

it hurts that you didn't even say goodbye

i spent months moving on, and
one small thing brings me back
to square one

- *i can't get over you*

does it scare you to think we may
forget each other's name one day?

you ain't never been in love until you
have begged God to help you let go

what if i never forget you?
what if, all my life,
when i meet someone new
i can never fall for them
because they aren't you?

a lot can happen in 6 months but
i never expected you to leave

we were. and then we weren't

i wish that you had stopped
saying you loved me
when you stopped meaning it

i always say i'm done with you
but i never am

i don't know how to stop loving you

- *things i realized when i understood*
- *you were never coming back*

you broke me but yet
i still think of you
as the greatest person
i have ever met
and that's how i know
that i truly love you

i never thought you'd be temporary

you can never say
i wasn't there for you
because i stayed
when i KNEW
i should've left

so loyal to you, i betrayed myself

we only obsess over relationships
that feel unfinished

i gave my all to someone
who didn't appreciate it

your name still breaks my heart

we are neither on
good terms or bad
we are no longer anything

i almost wish we never met

i was the one who loved you
even when you gave me
thousands of reasons
not to

but how do you let go
of the person that
felt like home?

do me a favor and don't come back
because i'll probably just let you
back in until you decide to leave again

you don't realize how long a year is
until you spend a year without someone

don't pretend like
this didn't mean
anything to you
i was there
i saw the way
you looked at me

and i'm afraid i will miss you forever

you had me at a point
where i would've left
the entire world behind
for you

i almost wish we never met

i was the one who loved you
even when you gave me
thousands of reasons
not to

but how do you let go
of the person that
felt like home?

do me a favor and don't come back
because i'll probably just let you
back in until you decide to leave again

you don't realize how long a year is
until you spend a year without someone

don't pretend like
this didn't mean
anything to you
i was there
i saw the way
you looked at me

and i'm afraid i will miss you forever

it's pathetic really, how much i still
hope it's you and me in the end

it hurts having you in my life
it hurts not having you in my life
i can't win

why did you say all those
things, if you weren't
planning on staying?

it's been months since i lost you
and yet it still hurts

you let go of me so easily

i knew you were gonna
break my heart
but a part of me
really hoped you
wouldn't

i will wait for you because
honestly i don't want anyone else

you and i were probably never
meant to be, but i loved every
single second that i spent with
you

how do you look at someone
you love and tell yourself
it's time to walk away?

i think what hurts is the fact
that i thought you felt the same

- *but you don't*

letting you go
was the hardest thing
i have ever done.
but not as hard as
watching you
not wanting me
for all that time

after all these months
it's still you, it was always you

i want you to know
that even though
we don't talk anymore
i still think about you
and the way things ended
and some nights
i still cry about it

i never wanted or longed for a goodbye
but when you left, it was all i could ask for

who knew one day we'd be an "*almost*"

don't you get it?
i can say goodbye
to everyone else
but not you
not you

you didn't deserve
how well i treated you
how long i stayed with you
how i would stay awake
just to speak to you

- you didn't deserve it

it hurts to wait for someone
who's never coming back

you will search for me
in another person, i promise

i still think about you a lot but
i don't wish for you to come back

i still get sad about
what happened
and how you left
every now and
then it just hits me
sometimes it takes
days for me
to get over it

you just don't get it, do you?
there is no undoing
what you have done

it's over, but in some ways
it isn't

it hurts, but i can't blame you
for not loving me back

if it doesn't destroy you when
it's over, then it wasn't love

because when everything else
felt wrong, you always felt right

and suddenly you were
everything i cared about

i'm sorry i mistook
all our laughs long nights,
sweet texts and inside jokes
as you caring about me
i'll think twice before
wasting my time again

the saddest part in life is saying
goodbye to someone you wish
to spend your lifetime with

you were the hardest lesson
i had to learn

i'd give anything just for you
to look at me the way you used to

the way our conversations
have changed breaks my heart

funny how losing someone ruins
your ability to love anyone else
just as deeply

i was starting to recover but
then you texted me again

you don't miss me
i should remember that
i should fucking remember that

what hurts is that we never really
said goodbye, we just kind of ended

i knew from the beginning
i wouldn't be able to keep you
but i tried anyway

do you know how many
times i've cried for you?

stop looking at me like
you want me because
we both know you don't

i wish i felt nothing
when i heard your name

you don't get it
i would've done anything
i would have thrown
everything away
just to be with you

i don't know how to
deal with your absence

your name hurts

i miss how close we were

i still remember how
we started talking

we don't talking anymore
and the saddest part is,
we used to talk everyday

you looked at me in the eyes
for a little too long to
"not have feelings for me"

our last goodbye was never said

nothing
made me sadder
than imagining
not seeing you
ever again

i think it will always hurt when
someone says your name

i knew you didn't love me
but i adored you anyway

you were my *"yes"*,
but i was only your *"maybe"*

i can't wait for the day when
you realize you fucked up

you didn't even tell me why
you just decided i wasn't
good enough for you
anymore and left

i'm really hoping you miss me too

you will always be my favorite "*almost*"

a part of me will always
wait for you to come back

i still repeat the things you said
to me in my head

can we please talk, for even
5 minutes, it's been over a month
and i miss you a lot

we flirted
we texted
we laughed
we cried
we stayed up just
to talk to each other
we said i love you...
now we don't talk at all

i miss you so fucking
much but i know that
you are fine without
me and i just wish
i was too

i'm over you
i'm over you
i'm over you
i'm over you
i'm over you
i'm over you
i'm over you

"*hey*"

... great, just great

i tried
you didn't
i cried
you didn't
you left
i didn't

i thought we'd have more time

you left
but never really
left,
does that make sense?

i know you don't feel the same way
but i really can't get over you

your eyes make me shy

a part of me still thinks that
if i find the right words,
it will save us

my mistake was making you a priority
when i was your second choice

i feel sick when i remember
how i opened up to you

i gave up because you never
once fought for me

it's sad when someone
can walk right past you and
pretend that you were never
a big part of their life

and one day your name
didn't make me smile anymore

i know you care about me but
i also know you don't care enough
and i don't know which is worse

you have no idea how badly i want
your name to light up on my phone

i hold onto every single memory because
i know we won't be making anymore

we're over now and the saddest
thing is, we never began

i wonder if we will ever talk
again like we used to

i hope one day you think of me and
wonder how you ever let me walk away

i have been staying awake at night,
wondering if i should tell you

i never would have expected
you to become my deepest
scar yet

i still have feelings for you
and no matter how many times
i tell myself i'm better off without
you, a part of me just won't let go

akhira

i don't care how complicated
this gets, i still want you

i got way too attached to you

the truth is,
if i could be with anyone
it'd still be you

i want to ask you, what i mean to you
but i'm afraid of the answer

i hope they ask you
about me
and i hope
you tell them
you fucked up

i hope my absence haunts you

the worst part is when you
start to question if they
even cared at all

a part of me
wants to move on
and forget you but
another part of me
wants to remember
you and how happy
you made me
at one point

i felt more with you
in the weeks we talked
than with someone
i spent years with

i will always have a thing for you

sometimes you can't explain
what you see in a person
it's just the way they take you
to a place no one else can

you and i were probably
never meant to be
but i loved every second
that i spent with you

you are still my favorite person

i hope you know
i pray for your happiness
like i pray for mine

and i'm afraid i will
love you forever

i will always want the best for you
even if we don't speak anymore

it hurts to be broken but
it hurts more when you're still in
love with the person who broke you

i think no matter how much time passes,
i will always have weak spot for you

you don't know heartbreak until
you're standing in front of the person
you love more than anything
knowing it's time to say goodbye

i knew i liked you when
you made me nervous
and my heart would
beat faster when i saw you
i knew i loved you when
i felt calmer with you
than without you

it's 2 in the morning
and i can't sleep
because every time
i close my eyes
i see versions of us
that could've
happened
if you didn't
leave

i said goodbye but my heart
was breaking

if you only knew how much those little
moments with you mattered to me

it still hurts because you
really meant something to me

it's been 8 months
and i still miss you

even if we make eye contact for a split
second, it means the world to me

and it makes me sad
that i don't cross your mind
when you are the reason
i lost mine

i always think of you
before i fall asleep
the words you said
the way you looked
the things we talked
about, the silent
moments we shared

\-   *i always think of you*

i will wait for you because
honestly i don't want anyone else

i miss you a lot more
than i realized
things keep
happening
and i always
find myself wishing
i could tell you
about them

i'm scared to move on because
moving on means accepting our
fate as strangers and i'd rather be
heartbroken than forget you

i guess... i just thought
eventually you would choose me
so i continuously chose you

a year ago you were here

every time someone tells me to
make a wish, i wish for you

you never thought you'd get
this attached, did you?

i'm sorry i wasn't enough to
make you stay in love with me

you broke me more than
anyone else, but if you
called me at 2 am in tears
saying you needed me
i'll be there for you
in a heartbeat and that
is the pain of loving
someone who
no longer
loves you

i had to get over
the fact that
i would probably
never get an apology
from you
because in your mind
you'd done absolutely
nothing wrong

no more tears, because
i didn't lose you, you lost me

i tell everyone i hate you
but i miss you so so much

i wish you knew how many nights
i stayed up wondering
why i wasn't good enough

i miss how you loved me

.

i wish you felt the same

tonight is just one of those nights
where i miss you terribly and
want to talk to you

all i ever wanted was for your name
to pop up on my phone saying
that you missed me

i still want you
no matter how much
time we spend apart or
how far away we are
from one and other
it's still you
it always will be

and it hurts to know someone
will love me, but someone isn't you

you don't know how deeply
in love you are with someone
until you try to walk away from them

i want nothing but the best for you
i really do, it's just that sometimes
i wish that the best for you was me

i didn't mean to fall in love
with you but i did
and you didn't mean
to hurt me but you did

i wish we could go back
in time to before it all
went wrong when we
were pointlessly flirting
and joking around
before i fell for you
before we broke
each other's hearts

they say it takes 21 days to break
a habit, but it's been 8 months
and i'm still in love with you

don't walk away and then say
i deserved better, i didn't want
better, i wanted you

sometimes the people we love
don't love us back
but that doesn't make
our love for them any less real
you could go as far as to say
it makes it more real
compared to loving someone
that you are with
you get used to them
you expect them to always be there
you start to appreciate them less
in contrary to loving someone
you can't be with
there is a deeper desire
and the feeling never goes away
it stays as an idea
and love
at it's essence
in its purity
is an idea
so when i say i love you
and you don't love me back
that's the highest form of love
there is

-   *unrequited love*

your name still hurts…

Made in United States
Troutdale, OR
10/16/2023